ACHIEVE LEVEL 6

Mathematics Revision

Hilary Koll and Steve Mills

RISING STARS

Rising Stars UK Ltd, 7 Hatchers Mews, Bermondsey Street,
London SE1 3GS
www.risingstars-uk.com

All facts are correct at time of going to press.

First published 2013
Reprinted with revisions 2013
This edition incorporating revisions 2014

Project manager: Dawn Booth
Editorial: Sue Walton
Proofreader: Bobby Francis
Design: Words & Pictures Ltd, London
Cover design: Marc Burville-Riley

British Library Cataloguing-in-Publication Data
A CIP record for this book is available from the British Library.

ISBN: 978-1-78339-421-0

Printed in India by Multivista Global Ltd

Contents

How to use this book

What we have included:

- Those topics at Level 5 that are trickiest to get right ('The tricky bits!').
- ALL Level 6 content so you know that you are covering all the topics that you need to understand in order to achieve Level 6.
- We have also put in a selection of our favourite test techniques, tips for revision and some advice on what the National Tests are all about, as well as the answers so you can see how well you are getting on.

(1) **Introduction** – This section tells you what you need to do to get to Level 6. It picks out the key learning objective and explains it simply to you.

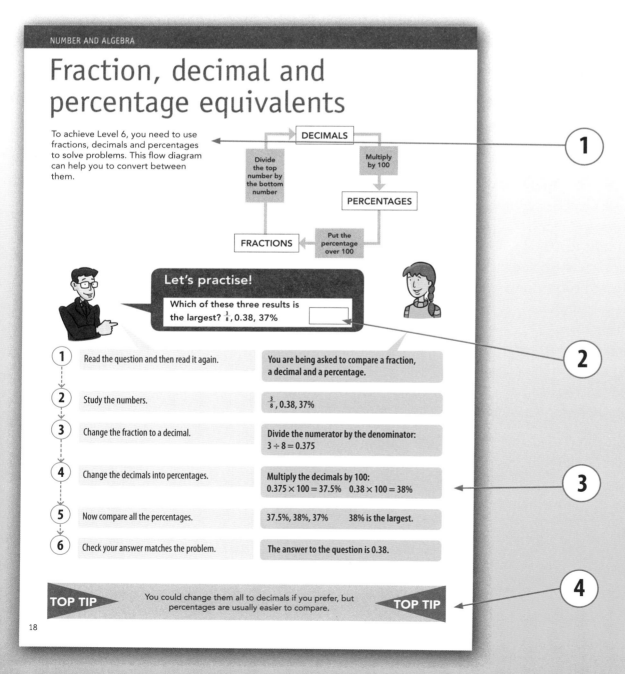

NUMBER AND ALGEBRA

Fraction, decimal and percentage equivalents

To achieve Level 6, you need to use fractions, decimals and percentages to solve problems. This flow diagram can help you to convert between them.

DECIMALS

Divide the top number by the bottom number

Multiply by 100

PERCENTAGES

Put the percentage over 100

FRACTIONS

(1)

Let's practise!

Which of these three results is the largest? $\frac{3}{8}$, 0.38, 37%

(2)

(1)	Read the question and then read it again.	You are being asked to compare a fraction, a decimal and a percentage.
(2)	Study the numbers.	$\frac{3}{8}$, 0.38, 37%
(3)	Change the fraction to a decimal.	Divide the numerator by the denominator: $3 \div 8 = 0.375$
(4)	Change the decimals into percentages.	Multiply the decimals by 100: $0.375 \times 100 = 37.5\%$ $0.38 \times 100 = 38\%$
(5)	Now compare all the percentages.	37.5%, 38%, 37% 38% is the largest.
(6)	Check your answer matches the problem.	The answer to the question is 0.38.

(3)

TOP TIP You could change them all to decimals if you prefer, but percentages are usually easier to compare. **TOP TIP**

(4)

18

(2) **Question** – The question helps you to learn by doing. It is presented in a similar way to a National Test question and gives you a real example to work with.

(3) **Flow chart** – This shows you the steps to use when completing questions like this. Some of the advice appears on every flow chart (e.g. 'Read the question then read it again'). This is because this is the best way of getting good marks in the National Tests.

(4) **Tip boxes** – These provide test hints and general tips on getting the best marks in the National Tests.

(5) **Practice questions** – This is where you have to do the work! Try each question using the technique in the flow chart then check your answers at the back. Practising questions is the best way to help improve your understanding.

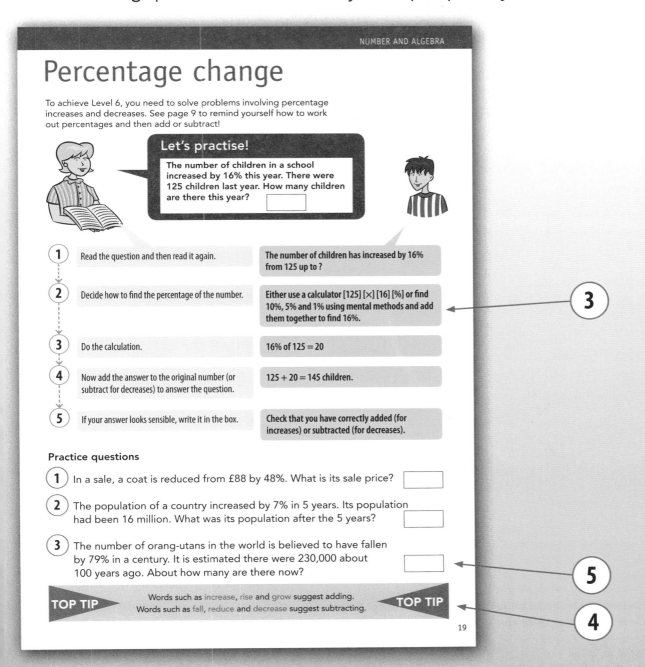

NUMBER AND ALGEBRA

Percentage change

To achieve Level 6, you need to solve problems involving percentage increases and decreases. See page 9 to remind yourself how to work out percentages and then add or subtract!

Let's practise!

The number of children in a school increased by 16% this year. There were 125 children last year. How many children are there this year?

(1) Read the question and then read it again. — The number of children has increased by 16% from 125 up to ?

(2) Decide how to find the percentage of the number. — Either use a calculator [125] [×] [16] [%] or find 10%, 5% and 1% using mental methods and add them together to find 16%.

(3) Do the calculation. — 16% of 125 = 20

(4) Now add the answer to the original number (or subtract for decreases) to answer the question. — 125 + 20 = 145 children.

(5) If your answer looks sensible, write it in the box. — Check that you have correctly added (for increases) or subtracted (for decreases).

Practice questions

(1) In a sale, a coat is reduced from £88 by 48%. What is its sale price?

(2) The population of a country increased by 7% in 5 years. Its population had been 16 million. What was its population after the 5 years?

(3) The number of orang-utans in the world is believed to have fallen by 79% in a century. It is estimated there were 230,000 about 100 years ago. About how many are there now?

TOP TIP Words such as increase, rise and grow suggest adding. Words such as fall, reduce and decrease suggest subtracting. **TOP TIP**

19

5

Key facts*

Place value

The position of a digit in a number gives its value.

Ten thousands	Thousands	Hundreds	Tens	Units	Tenths	Hundredths	
40,000 +	7000 +	300 +	20 +	7 +	0.6 +	0.04	= 47,327.64

Rounding

Remember that 5 is rounded upwards, so 48.25 rounds up to 48.3.

Positive and negative integers

Integers are just whole numbers.

Remember to count 0 when counting from negative to positive and vice versa.

Properties of number

Square: the number made when a number is multiplied by itself.

Multiple: numbers in a number's times table. For example, some multiples of 3 are 3, 6, 36, 72 and 147.

Common multiples: multiples that are the same for different numbers. For example, 12 is a common multiple of 2, 3, 4, 6 and 12.

Factors: numbers that divide into another number without leaving a remainder. For example, the factors of 12 are 1, 2, 3, 4, 6 and 12.

Prime numbers: a number that has just two factors – itself and 1.

Tests of divisibility

A number can be divided by	If
2	it is even.
3	the sum of its digits is divisible by 3.
4	its last two digits are divisible by 4.
5	it ends in 5 or 0.
6	it is divisible by 2 and 3.
7	no 'ifs'. You have to work this one out the hard way!
8	half of the number can be divided by 4.
9	the sum of its digits is divisible by 9.
10	it ends in 0.

Fractions

Numerators tell us how many equal parts we have.

Denominators tell us how many equal parts there are.

Simplifying fractions

To simplify a fraction to its simplest form (or lowest terms) you need to find a common factor you can divide into both the numerator and the denominator. For example, to simplify $\frac{12}{16}$ divide the numerator and the denominator by 4: $\frac{12}{16} = \frac{3}{4}$

When multiplying fractions, multiply the numerators together, then multiply the denominators together and then simplify. For example, $\frac{3}{5} \times \frac{5}{6} = \frac{15}{30} = \frac{1}{2}$ (You can diagonally cancel first if it is easier.)

* Important note for Teachers and Parents: These key facts relate to the Primary Mathematics Framework (2006) because pupils in Year 6 will continue to be taught and assessed against it in the academic year 2014–15.

Fraction, decimal and percentage equivalents

Remember these equivalents:

Fraction	$\frac{1}{2}$	$\frac{1}{4}$	$\frac{1}{10}$	$\frac{3}{4}$	$\frac{1}{3}$
Decimal	0.5	0.25	0.1	0.75	0.33 (approximately)
Percentage	50%	25%	10%	75%	33% (approximately)

Ratio and proportion

Ratio is 'to every'. **Proportion** is 'for every' and can be given as a fraction, decimal or percentage.

You should simplify ratios and proportions to their simplest form.

Checking answers

Inverse means opposite. Check addition by subtraction and vice versa. Check multiplication by division and vice versa.

Addition and subtraction of decimals

Line up the decimal points when you write out the calculation.

Fill any empty spaces with a 0. Remember to put the decimal point in the answer.

Brackets

Always do the brackets in equations first.

Sometimes the mnemonic **BODMAS** is used to remind you that you do **b**rackets first, then **o**ther things like squaring or powers, then **d**ivision and **m**ultiplication and finally **a**ddition and **s**ubtraction.

2-D shapes

Perpendicular lines make a right angle. Parallel lines never meet. They can be straight or curved.

Triangles

Equilateral triangles have three equal sides and three equal angles. **Isosceles triangles** have two equal sides and two equal angles. **Scalene triangles** have three sides of different length and three angles of different sizes. **Right-angled triangles** can be isosceles or scalene.

Transforming 2-D shapes

When you draw reflections, remember to keep the correct distance from the mirror line. Rotational symmetry is about how many ways a shape can fit exactly on top of itself. When translating a shape move it across first and then up or down.

Coordinates

Always read along the x-axis and then up or down the y-axis.

Always write x before y, i.e. (x and y).

Approximate metric and imperial conversions

1 litre = 1.8 pints
1 mile = 1.6 km
1 metre = 3 feet 3 inches
Centi = $\frac{1}{100}$

1 kilogram = 2.2 lbs (pounds)
5 miles = 8 km
1 inch = 2.5 cm
Cent = 100

1 pound = 0.454 kg
1 foot = 30 cm
Milli = $\frac{1}{1000}$
Kilo = 1000

Area of a rectangle

Area of a rectangle = length (*l*) × width (*w*)

Averages

Mean is the sum of all values divided by the number of values.
Median is the middle value when a list of values has been written in order.
Mode is the most common value.
Range is the difference between the highest and lowest value.

About the National Tests

Key facts

You take Key Stage 2 National Tests in the summer term in Year 6. If you take the Level 6 mathematics test you will also take the Level 3–5 test. The Level 6 mathematics National Test consists of two papers:

• Paper 1 is a non-calculator paper, lasting 30 minutes.

• Paper 2 is a calculator available paper, lasting 30 minutes.

The papers include harder Level 5 questions as well as Level 6 questions.

The Level 5 questions usually ask you to use and apply skills (such as how to engage with a problem, complete an appropriate method, and interpret and reflect on outcomes).

Your marks from both papers will be combined to decide whether or not you are working at Level 6 in mathematics.

Using and applying mathematics

The Level 6 papers will include lots of questions that involve using and applying your mathematical knowledge and skills. You will be given marks for explaining your reasoning, setting your work out clearly, checking your results and using symbols and diagrams to describe things mathematically. Most of this book helps you to practise for these questions. On pages 57 to 59 you will find more help with these skills.

Calculating percentages of amounts

At Level 5 you need to calculate simple percentages of numbers and quantities.

Let's practise!
Without a calculator

61% of 4200 people at a concert were women. How many were women?

1 Read the question and then read it again. | **Find how many of the people are women.**

2 First find 50% of the total number of people. | 50% of 4200 = 2100

3 Then find 10% by dividing by 10. | 10% of 4200 = 420

4 Next find 1% by dividing by 100 and then add the answers together. | 1% of 4200 = 42
2100 + 420 + 42 = 2562

5 Does your answer seem sensible? | **2562 women out of 4200 people is over one half and seems to be about 60% of the whole.**

Let's practise!
The example below shows how you can use your calculator to find a percentage of number or quantity.

James was given a bonus of 27% of his salary. His salary is £16,500. How much was his bonus?

1 Read the question and then read it again. | **Find 27% of 16,500.**

2 Make an estimate of the answer. | 27% is about $\frac{1}{4}$. $\frac{1}{4}$ of £16,500 is just over £4000.

3 Key in the numbers on the calculator. | [16,500] [×] [27] [%]

4 Does your answer seem sensible? If so, write it in the box. | **The answer is 4455 which is close to our estimate. Redo the calculation to check it.**

Negative numbers

To achieve Level 5, you need to understand negative numbers. These are just like positive numbers but on the other side of zero.

Let's practise!

Overnight the temperature drops from 4°C to –9°C.
By how many degrees did it fall?

1 Read the question and then read it again.

You must find the difference between 4 and –9

2 Picture the numbers.

One is positive and one is negative. Sketch a simple number line:

–9   0   4

3 Count up or back, using zero as a stop-over point.

From –9 to zero is 9 and from zero to 4 is 4:
9 + 4 = 13

4 Check your calculation.

Count back 13 from 4. Do you reach –9?

5 Does your answer seem sensible? If so, write it in the box.

If not, go back to step 3 and try again.

Practice questions

1 The temperature rises from –15°C to 12°C.
By how many degrees did it rise?

2 The temperature falls from 14°C to –7°C.
By how many degrees did it fall?

3 What is the difference between –8°C and 9°C?

TOP TIP   Whole numbers are sometimes called integers. Don't let this put
you off. It just means numbers that are not decimals or fractions.
These numbers are integers: –5, 4, 7, –11.
These numbers are not integers: 4.5, $3\frac{1}{2}$, 28.1.   **TOP TIP**

Long division

To achieve Level 5, you need to conquer long division.

Let's practise!

Write in the missing number.
798 ÷ 14 =

1	Read the question and then read it again.	798 ÷ 14 = ?
2	Picture the numbers.	**798 rounds up to 800 and 14 rounds down to 10.**
3	Study the numbers and think about them.	**798 ÷ 14 will be less than 800 ÷ 10 = 80.**

4   Set out the calculation and work out the first part, looking at the first two digits of the larger number to begin with.

```
      5
14 | 798
   -70
     9
```

Write some jottings to help you
2 × 14 = 28
3 × 14 = 42
4 × 14 = 56
5 × 14 = 70 …

5   Bring the next digit down and divide again.

```
     57
14 | 798
   -70
     98
   -98
      0
```

6 × 14 = 84
7 × 14 = 98 …

The answer is 57.

6   Check your answer. If it looks sensible, write it in the box.

You could multiply your answer by 14 to check you get 798.

Practice questions

1   768 ÷ 16 =

2   864 ÷ 24 =

3   918 ÷ 27 =

TOP TIP   For step 4, some people work out multiples of 10 and take the number as a whole. For example, they find 50 × 14 = 700 and then subtract 700 from 798. Either way is OK, so long as you get the correct answer!   **TOP TIP**

Multiplying and dividing decimals

To achieve Level 5, you need to work with decimal numbers. When multiplying and dividing decimals, you have to know where the decimal point goes!

Let's practise!

Write in the missing number
5.27 × 3.9 =

1 Read the question and then read it again.

$5.27 \times 3.9 = ?$

2 Picture the numbers.

They are nearly 5×4 which is about 20.

3 Study the numbers again and think about them.

The answer will be more than 15 (5×3) and less than 24 (6×4).

4 Calculate.

Imagine the question is 527×39 (without the decimal points) and work out the answer.

```
      527
   ×   39
   15,810
 + 4,743
   20,553
```

5 Compare the answer with your estimate.

Your answer should be about 20 (between 15 and 24) so it must be 20.553, rather than 2.0553 or 205.53, etc.

6 Check that the number of digits after the decimal points in the question is the same as the number in your answer.

$5.27 \times 3.9 = 20.553$
(There are three digits in the question and three are in the answer!)

7 Does your answer seem sensible? If it does, write it in the box!

If not, go back to step 4 and try again.

TOP TIP

Be careful with the rule about the number of decimal places in the question and answer, as it only works for multiplication! When dividing, use your estimates to decide where to put the decimal point.

TOP TIP

Formulae

Formulae can be written in words or using letters. To achieve Level 5, you may have to write formulae yourself.

Let's practise!

At a funfair there is a £5 entrance fee and then each ride costs £2. Write a formula to show the total cost *T* in pounds for entering the funfair and then going on *N* rides.

1	Read the question and then read it again.	You must write a formula for the total cost using the letters *N* and *T*.
2	Study the numbers and write out what you know.	*T* = total cost Entrance fee = £5 Each ride = £2 Number of rides = *N*
3	Say the formula in words.	The total cost is the entrance fee £5 plus *N* lots of £2.
4	Write out your formula using letters.	$T = 5 + N \times 2$ (As *T* is the total cost in pounds you don't need to use the £ sign.)
5	Think about whether it can be written more simply.	$T = 5 + 2N$

Practice question

1 Jake buys a TV. He makes a first payment of £50 and then pays £20 each month to pay the rest. Write a formula to show the total price *P* in pounds for the TV if he pays for *N* months.

TOP TIP

Talk through your formula in your head. Think clearly. Take it step-by-step.
If a number and a letter are next to each other, for example 2*N*, it means they are multiplied. Why is the × (multiply) symbol left out? Because it could get confused with the letter x!

TOP TIP

Ratio and proportion

To achieve Level 5, you need to simplify ratios and proportions.
This is sometimes called **cancelling**.

Let's practise!

Look at this coloured rod.
What is the ratio of red to white sections?

1	Read the question and then read it again.	You need to find the ratio.
2	Count the red and white sections.	There are 12 red sections and 8 white ones.
3	What is the ratio of red to white sections?	red:white is 12:8.
4	Can you simplify (cancel) the ratio?	12 and 8 can be divided by 4 so 12:8 = 3:2

Let's practise!

Look again at the rod.
What proportion of the rod is red?

1	Read the question and then read it again.	You need to find the proportion (or fraction) that is red.
2	Count the red sections and count the total number of sections.	There are 12 red sections and a total of 20 sections.
3	What is the proportion of red sections?	Write this as a fraction: $\frac{12}{20}$
4	Can you simplify (cancel) the fraction?	12 and 20 can be divided by 4 so $\frac{12}{20} = \frac{3}{5}$ or 3 out of 5. The answer is 3 out of 5 rods are red.

Areas and perimeters of rectangles

To achieve Level 5, you need to know how to find the perimeters and areas of rectangles. It's easy – just remember these formulae:

the perimeter of a rectangle = 2 × (the length plus the width) or $P = 2(l + w)$
the area of a rectangle = the length × the width or $A = l \times w$

Let's practise!

Find the perimeter and area of this rectangle.

$P =$ $A =$

5 cm

10 cm

1	Read the question and then read it again.	You are being asked to find the perimeter and the area.
2	Write what you know.	The length is 10 cm and the width is 5 cm.
3	Remember the formula for the perimeter.	$P = 2(l + w)$
4	Find the perimeter of the rectangle and write the correct unit of measurement.	$P = 2 \times (10 + 5)$ $P = 2 \times 15 = 30$ $P = 30$ cm
5	Remember the formula for the area.	$A = l \times w$
6	Find the area of the rectangle and write the unit of measurement.	$A = 10 \times 5 = 50$ $A = 50$ cm²
7	If your answers look sensible, write them in the boxes.	If not, go back to step 2 and try again.

TOP TIPS

When dealing with perimeter, make sure the units are lengths, for example cm, m, km.
When dealing with area, make sure the units are always squared, for example cm², m², km².

Adding and subtracting fractions and mixed numbers

To achieve Level 6, you need to be able to add, subtract and compare fractions by changing them so that they have a common denominator.

Let's practise!

Give your answer as a mixed number:

$\frac{7}{8} + \frac{1}{6} = $ ⬚

1 Read the question and then read it again.

Take note: denominators (bottom numbers) of the fractions are not the same! You must change the fractions to equivalent ones with the same denominators before you can add or subtract.

2 Find the smallest number that both denominators divide into (the lowest common multiple).

8 and 6 both divide into 24, so 24 will be the new denominator.

3 Begin to rewrite the fractions as equivalent ones. Write out the numbers with the new denominator under a long line.

$\frac{7}{8} + \frac{1}{6} = \frac{}{24}$
You could write 24 twice, once for each fraction, but writing it once saves time!

4 Work out the first new numerator.

How many 8s in 24? 3, so multiply the numerator, 7, by 3 to give 21.
$\frac{7}{8} + \frac{1}{6} = \frac{21+}{24}$

5 Work out the second numerator and then add the two together (or subtract if the question is a subtraction).

How many 6s in 24? 4, so multiply the numerator, 1, by 4 to give 4.
$\frac{7}{8} + \frac{1}{6} = \frac{21+4}{24} = \frac{25}{24}$. Only add on top!

6 Reread the question. Simplify the fraction if you can and write it in the form asked for.

$\frac{25}{24} = 1\frac{1}{24}$

7 If your answer looks sensible, write it in the box.

If not, go back to step 2 and try again.

TOP TIP To change fractions to equivalent ones, multiply or divide the numerator and the denominator by the same number, for example $\frac{3}{8} = \frac{6}{16} = \frac{9}{24}$ **TOP TIP**

Practice questions

1 $\frac{4}{5} + \frac{1}{3} =$ ☐

2 $\frac{5}{6} - \frac{1}{4} =$ ☐

3 $\frac{4}{7} + \frac{3}{5} =$ ☐

4 $\frac{4}{5} - \frac{3}{8} =$ ☐

5 $\frac{3}{5} - \frac{4}{7} =$ ☐

6 $\frac{4}{5} + \frac{3}{8} =$ ☐

Sometimes you must add or subtract mixed numbers.

Adding is easy! Add the fractions first and then add on the whole numbers.

With subtraction it is usually easier to rewrite the mixed numbers as improper (top-heavy) fractions.

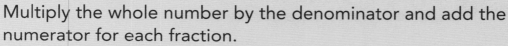

Example question

$2\frac{1}{6} - 1\frac{2}{3} =$ ☐

Multiply the whole number by the denominator and add the numerator for each fraction.
$2 \times 6 + 1 = 13, \quad 1 \times 3 + 2 = 5$
13 and 5 are the new numerators.

This is because 2 wholes $= \frac{12}{6}$
so $2\frac{1}{6} = \frac{13}{6}$ and 1 whole $= \frac{3}{3}$ so $1\frac{2}{3} = \frac{5}{3}$

So now answer the question $\frac{13}{6} - \frac{5}{3}$ instead!

Practice questions

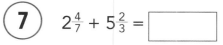

7 $2\frac{4}{7} + 5\frac{2}{3} =$ ☐

8 $4\frac{2}{5} - 1\frac{7}{10} =$ ☐

9 $5\frac{2}{3} - 3\frac{4}{5} =$ ☐

10 $6\frac{1}{4} - 3\frac{5}{8} =$ ☐

TOP TIP   If two fractions have the same denominator you can add or subtract them easily. All you do is add the numerator! Don't add the denominators – they stay the same! $\frac{25}{24} + \frac{5}{24} = \frac{30}{24}$ (not $\frac{30}{48}$).   **TOP TIP**

Fraction, decimal and percentage equivalents

To achieve Level 6, you need to use fractions, decimals and percentages to solve problems. This flow diagram can help you to convert between them.

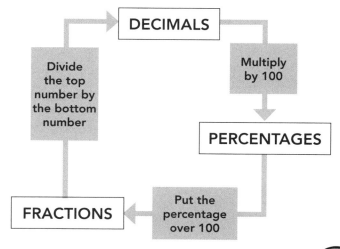

DECIMALS

Divide the top number by the bottom number

Multiply by 100

PERCENTAGES

Put the percentage over 100

FRACTIONS

Let's practise!

Which of these three results is the largest? $\frac{3}{8}$, 0.38, 37%

1 Read the question and then read it again.

You are being asked to compare a fraction, a decimal and a percentage.

2 Study the numbers.

$\frac{3}{8}$, 0.38, 37%

3 Change the fraction to a decimal.

Divide the numerator by the denominator:
$3 \div 8 = 0.375$

4 Change the decimals into percentages.

Multiply the decimals by 100:
$0.375 \times 100 = 37.5\%$ $0.38 \times 100 = 38\%$

5 Now compare all the percentages.

37.5%, 38%, 37%   38% is the largest.

6 Check your answer matches the problem.

The answer to the question is 0.38.

TOP TIP   You could change them all to decimals if you prefer, but percentages are usually easier to compare.   **TOP TIP**

Percentage change

To achieve Level 6, you need to solve problems involving percentage increases and decreases. See page 9 to remind yourself how to work out percentages and then add or subtract!

Let's practise!

The number of children in a school increased by 16% this year. There were 125 children last year. How many children are there this year?

1	Read the question and then read it again.	The number of children has increased by 16% from 125 up to ?
2	Decide how to find the percentage of the number.	Either use a calculator [125] [×] [16] [%] or find 10%, 5% and 1% using mental methods and add them together to find 16%.
3	Do the calculation.	16% of 125 = 20
4	Now add the answer to the original number (or subtract for decreases) to answer the question.	125 + 20 = 145 children.
5	If your answer looks sensible, write it in the box.	Check that you have correctly added (for increases) or subtracted (for decreases).

Practice questions

1 In a sale, a coat is reduced from £88 by 48%. What is its sale price?

2 The population of a country increased by 7% in 5 years. Its population had been 16 million. What was its population after the 5 years?

3 The number of orang-utans in the world is believed to have fallen by 79% in a century. It is estimated there were 230,000 about 100 years ago. About how many are there now?

TOP TIP ▶ Words such as increase, rise and grow suggest adding.
Words such as fall, reduce and decrease suggest subtracting. ◀ **TOP TIP**

Writing a number as a fraction or percentage of another

To achieve Level 6, you need to be able to solve problems where you find one number as a fraction or percentage of another. The important question to ask is always, 'What is the whole in this problem?' otherwise you can easily get answers wrong.

Let's practise!

A dress is reduced by £10 in a sale. It now costs £70. By what fraction of the original price was the dress reduced?

What percentage reduction is this?

1 Read the questions and then read them again.

There is a lot to think about here!

2 Decide what is the whole. Is it the original price or the new price?

The whole here is the original price of the dress which you must work out first. £70 + £10 = £80

3 Write a fraction with the reduction on top and the whole below and then simplify the fraction.

Reduction = £10
Original price (the whole) = £80 $\frac{10}{80} = \frac{1}{8}$

4 Convert the fraction to a percentage.

Divide the numerator by the denominator and multiply by 100: $1 \div 8 \times 100 = 12.5\%$
Or you could use the % button on a calculator by pressing [1] [÷] [8] [%] [=]

5 If your answers look sensible, write them in the boxes.

It is worth finding $\frac{1}{8}$ of £80 and 12.5% of £80 to check that you get the reduction £10 each time.

Practice questions

1 **a)** A coat is reduced by £15 in a sale. It now costs £45. By what fraction of the original price was it reduced?

b) What percentage reduction is this?

2 **a)** A car's value in 2012 was £2400. In 2008 it had been worth £600 more. By what fraction of its value in 2008 had it dropped by 2012?

b) What percentage reduction is this?

3 **a)** Mr Jones was given a pay rise of £600. His new salary is £15,600 per year. By what fraction of his old salary did it rise?

b) What percentage increase is this?

Sometimes you need to work out how much the reduction or rise is by finding the difference first.

Example question

A car's value in 2008 was £3000. By 2012 its value had dropped to £1200. By what fraction of its value in 2008 had it dropped?

What percentage reduction is this?

The reduction can be found by subtracting £1200 from £3000. So £1800 is the reduction and the whole is £3000. Now use this information to answer the above questions.

Practice questions (continued)

4 **a)** A house's value was £125,000 in 2008. In 2012 its value was £175,000. By what fraction of its value in 2008 had it increased in 2012?

b) What percentage rise is this?

5 **a)** Mrs Jennings started a diet weighing 96 kg. By the end of her diet she weighed 84 kg. What fraction of her weight did she lose?

b) What percentage decrease is this?

TOP TIP Always check your answers by finding the fraction and percentage of the original amount to see if it gives the increase or decrease. **TOP TIP**

Using ratios to divide amounts

To achieve Level 6, you need to be able to use ratios to divide amounts or quantities. We don't always want to share things out equally, so ratios are used to say how the whole should be split up!

Let's practise!

A boss wants to split £210 between three of his workers, Donny, Ronnie and Jonny, in the ratio 2:3:5. How much will they each get?

1	Read the question and then read it again.	£210 is to be split into the ratio 2:3:5, which is two parts, three parts and five parts.
2	Add the parts of the ratio to find a total.	$2{:}3{:}5 \rightarrow 2 + 3 + 5 = 10$ parts altogether.
3	Divide the amount by this total to find out what one part is worth.	$£210 \div 10 = £21$, so one part is worth £21.
4	Multiply each number in the ratio by the one part.	$2 \times £21 = £42$, $3 \times £21 = £63$, $5 \times £21 = £105$
5	Check that the answers add up to the original amount.	$£42 + £63 + £105 = £210$
6	If they do and seem sensible, write them in the boxes.	If not, go back to step 2 and try again.

Practice questions

1. Split £54 into the ratio 1:2:3.

2. Split £280 into the ratio 3:4:7.

TOP TIP Remember: ADMC – add to find the total number of parts. Divide to find the value of one part. Then multiply for each number in the ratio. Finally, check by adding the answers. **TOP TIP**

Proportional reasoning

To achieve Level 6, you need to solve problems involving ratios and proportions. Proportional problems usually involve dividing and then multiplying (sometimes called scaling up or down).

Let's practise!

Eight ice creams cost £9.60. What would be the cost of five ice creams?

1	Read the question and then read it again.	You know the cost of eight ice creams and you need to find the cost of five of them.
2	Divide to find the cost of one.	£9.60 ÷ 8 = £1.20. Each ice cream costs £1.20.
3	Multiply to find the cost of several.	To find the cost for five, multiply £1.20 by 5: £1.20 × 5 = £6
4	Study the numbers and think about them.	Does it seem about right that eight ice creams cost £9.60 and five cost £6.00?
5	If your answer looks sensible, write it in the box.	If not, go back to step 2 and try again.

Practice questions

1 A machine takes 16 minutes to make 560 ping pong balls. At this rate, how many would it make in 30 minutes?

2 A recipe for 12 cakes uses 800 g of flour. How much flour would be needed for making 15 of these cakes?

3 A runner jogs at a constant rate for 65 minutes. If he ran 13 km in that time, how far had he run after 17 minutes?

TOP TIP Remember: divide to find one. Then multiply to find many. **TOP TIP**

Adding and subtracting negative numbers

For Level 6, you need to begin to understand how negative numbers can be used in calculations. (See page 10 for some revision first.) When you add or subtract negative numbers, two signs can appear next to each other, like these:

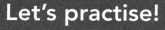

$1 - -3 =$

subtraction sign   the number –3

$-3 + -4 =$

addition sign   the number –4

If this happens, just follow these rules :

$- -$ think of as a $+$
$+ -$ think of as a $-$

Let's practise!

Add –5 and –9.

1   Read the question and then read it again.

Write it using symbols: $-5 + -9 = ?$

2   Which signs are next to each other? Remember the rule.

$+ -$ think of as a $-$

3   Write the question again, replacing the two signs next to each other with just one.

$-5 + -9 = ?$
$-5 - 9 = ?$

4   Do the calculation.

$-5 - 9 = -14$

Let's practise!

Find 10 subtract –6.

1   Read the question and then read it again.

Write it using symbols: $10 - -6 = ?$

2   Which signs are next to each other? Remember the rule.

$- -$ think of as a $+$

3   Write the question again, replacing the two signs next to each other with just one.

$10 - -6 = ?$
$10 + 6 = ?$

4   Do the calculation.

$10 + 6 = 16$

Using formulae

To achieve Level 6, you need to be able to substitute values into formulae. To substitute means to swap, like when a player is substituted in a football game.

Let's practise!

This formula shows how you can convert temperatures given in degrees Celsius (C) to degrees Fahrenheit (F). Find 15° Celsius in degrees Fahrenheit.

$F = (9C \div 5) + 32$

1	Read the question and then read it again.	Substitute the temperature given in place of C in the formula to find F.
2	Write out the formula in full.	Remember 9C means 9 × C. $F = (9 \times C \div 5) + 32$
3	Write which letter in the formula you know the value of.	C is 15.
4	Substitute the given value into the formula.	$F = (9 \times C \div 5) + 32$ $F = (9 \times 15 \div 5) + 32$
5	Calculate the value of the other letter.	$F = 27 + 32 = 59$
6	Write in your unit of measurement.	$F = 59°$ Fahrenheit.
7	If your answer looks sensible, write it in the box.	If not, go back to step 2 and try again.

Practice questions

1 Use the formula above to find 25° Celsius in degrees Fahrenheit.

2 Use the formula $s = 3t + 1$ to find the value of s when t is 6.

25

Trial and improvement

To achieve Level 6, you need to be able to use a strategy called 'trial and improvement' to get closer to an answer. It's easy – you start by guessing a number and trying it. If it's too large, you pick a smaller number to try. If it's too small you pick a larger number and so on. It's that simple!

Let's practise!

Solve $x^2 + x - 5 = 48$
to 1 decimal place (1dp).

1 Read the question and then read it again.	Solving means finding the value of x which makes the equation true.
2 Study the numbers and start to draw a table.	If $x =$ / then $x^2 + x - 5$ equals / which is
3 Pick a number to start and fill in the table. (You can use a calculator!)	(table below)

If $x =$	then $x^2 + x - 5$ equals	which is
10	$100 + 10 - 5 = 105$	too large
5	$25 + 5 - 5 = 25$	too small
7	$49 + 7 - 5 = 51$	too large
6.5	$42.25 + 6.5 - 5 = 43.75$	too small
6.7	$44.89 + 6.7 - 5 = 46.59$	too small
6.8	$46.24 + 6.8 - 5 = 48.04$	too large

4 Reread the question.	We could keep going but the question says to give your answer to 1 decimal place. The exact answer is between 6.7 and 6.8 but 6.8 is closer.
5 Check your answer matches the problem.	Put 6.8 into the equation again to check. $6.8^2 + 6.8 - 5 = 48.04$ which is close to 48.
6 If your answer looks sensible, write it in the box.	If not, go back to step 2 and try again.

TOP TIP The aim is to find a number that gets you as close as possible to the answer given, here 48. **TOP TIP**

Practice questions

1 Solve $x^2 - x + 3 = 16$ to 1 decimal place.
Draw a table that starts like this:

If x =	then $x^2 - x + 3$ equals	which is

2 Solve $x^2 + 3x = 15.4$ to 1 decimal place.
Draw a table that starts like this:

If x =	then $x^2 + (3 \times x)$ equals	which is

Sometimes the equation may contain a cubed number, for example x^3 or $x \times x \times x$.

When using a calculator, if there is a $[x^3]$ use it, or press the number and then $[\wedge]$ and $[3]$ to cube it, or use the multiplication button to do $x \times x \times x$.

Example question
Solve $x^3 + x = 116$ to 1 decimal place.

If x =	then $x^3 + x$ equals	which is
5	125 + 5 = 130	too large
4	64 + 4 = 68	too small
4.5	91.125 + 4.5 = 95.625	too small
4.7	103.823 + 4.7 = 108.523	too small
4.8	110.592 + 4.8 = 115.392	too small
4.9	117.649 + 4.9 = 122.549	too large

The answer is between 4.8 and 4.9 but which gives the answer closer to 116?

Practice questions (continued)

3 Solve $x^3 - x = 4$ to 1 decimal place.
Draw a table that starts like this:

If x =	then $x^3 - x$ equals	which is

TOP TIP Compare each answer you get with the answer given in the equation. **TOP TIP**

Solving simple linear equations

To achieve Level 6, you need to solve linear equations by finding the value of the letter or missing value.

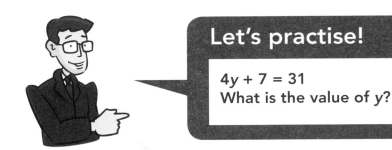 

Let's practise!

$4y + 7 = 31$
What is the value of y?

1	Read the question and then read it again.	To solve this equation find out what y is worth.
2	Study the equation and say it in words.	*'If I multiply y by 4 and then add 7, I get 31.'*
3	Keep the equation balanced by adding or subtracting the same from both sides of the equals sign. Try to make the equation simpler.	$4y + 7 = 31$ $4y + 7 - 7 = 31 - 7$ $4y = 24$
4	Look at your simpler equation. What does it mean?	**4 lots of y equals 24**
5	Divide both sides by the same number to find the value of the letter.	$4y = 24$ $4y \div 4 = 24 \div 4$ $y = 6$
6	Check your answer by rereading step 2, inserting the number for the letter.	*'If I multiply 6 by 4 and add 7 I get 31.'*
7	If your answer looks sensible, write it in the box.	**If not, go back to step 2 and try again.**

TOP TIP
Think of the equation as a set of balance scales. What is on one side is equal to the other. Whatever you do, do the same to both sides and it will still balance.
If a number and a letter are next to each other, for example 2N, it means they are multiplied.
TOP TIP

Practice questions

1 $2y + 4 = 18$ What is the value of y?   ☐

2 $5r - 6 = 4$ What is the value of r?   ☐

3 $6n - 12 = 30$ What is the value of n?   ☐

4 $62 = 8m + 6$ What is the value of m?   ☐

Sometimes a linear equation has letters on both sides. If this is the case, don't worry! Just collect the letters together on one side of the equals sign and the numbers on the other.

Let's practise!

$9x - 21 = 2x + 14$
What is the value of x? ☐

1 Read the equation and then say it in words.

'If I multiply x by 9 and subtract 21 I get the same answer as if I multiply x by 2 and add 14.'

2 Keep the equation balanced by adding or subtracting the same from both sides of the equals sign. Try to make the equation simpler.

$$9x - 21 = 2x + 14$$
$$9x - 21 + 21 = 2x + 14 + 21$$
$$9x = 2x + 35$$
$$9x - 2x = 2x - 2x + 35$$
$$7x = 35$$

3 Divide both sides by the same number to find the value of the letter.

$$7x = 35$$
$$7x \div 7 = 35 \div 7$$
$$x = 5$$

4 Check by rereading step 1 inserting the number for the letter.

'If I multiply 5 by 9 and then subtract 21 I get 24. If I multiply 5 by 2 and then add 14 I get 24.'

5 If your answer looks sensible, write it in the box.

If not, go back to step 1 and try again.

Practice questions (continued)

5 $5y - 18 = 2y + 3$ What is the value of y?   ☐

6 $6m + 4 = 9m - 14$ What is the value of m?   ☐

29

Expanding brackets

To achieve Level 6, you need to know how to expand brackets by multiplying everything inside the bracket by what is outside the bracket. It's easy to forget to multiply everything so draw arcs above to remind you!

$$4(x + 2) = 4 \times x + 4 \times 2 = 4x + 8$$

Let's practise!

Expand $5(y - 3)$ [ ]

1 Read the question and then read it again.

2 Draw arcs to remind you what to multiply.

3 Simplify the expression.

4 If your answer looks sensible, write it in the box.

To expand or open the brackets, multiply what is on the outside by everything inside.

$5(y - 3) = 5 \times y - 5 \times 3$

$5 \times y - 5 \times 3 = 5y - 15$

If not, go back to step 2 and try again.

Practice questions

1 Expand $3(4 + m)$ [ ]

2 Expand $7(y + z)$ [ ]

3 Expand $4(2a + 3b)$ [ ]

4 Expand $5(2m - 7)$ [ ]

You might be asked to **solve** an equation that has brackets.

Example question
Solve $3(x + 4) = 15$ [ ]
Expand the brackets and solve in the normal way
(see pages 28 and 29).

Practice questions (continued)

5 Solve $2(m + 3) = 14$ [ ]

6 Solve $6(2y + 1) = 42$ [ ]

Finding a rule for the nth term of a sequence

To achieve Level 6, you need to be able to describe sequences and find a rule that will show how any term in the sequence can be found. It sounds difficult but it isn't, as long as you follow the steps!

Let's practise!

Write a rule for the nth term of this sequence:
5, 8, 11, 14, 17, 20, 23, 26... .

(1) Read the question and then read it again.

You must give a rule to show how any term of the sequence can be found.

(2) Write out the terms of the sequence.

5	8	11	14	17	20	23	26

(3) Find the difference between the terms. If this number is always the same, it tells you which times table is related to the sequence.

5	8	11	14	17	20	23	26
3	3	3	3	3	3	3	

The rule is related to the 3 times table or '$3n$'.

(4) Write out the times table, for example $3n$.

The 3 times table or $3n$ is:

3	6	9	12	15	18	21	24

(5) Ask 'How many must I add or subtract to this times table to make the sequence in the question?'

Notice that you must add 2 to each term in the times table $3n$ to get the sequence 5, 8, 11 ...

(6) Write this rule in words.

The rule for the nth term of this sequence is: multiply by 3 and add 2. This can also be written as $3n + 2$.

(7) Check your answer by inserting 1, then 2, then 3 ...

$3n + 2$ (term 1) $3 \times 1 + 2 = 5$
(term 2) $3 \times 2 + 2 = 8$
(term 3) $3 \times 3 + 2 = 11$ ...

TOP TIP ▶ Rules can be written in words or in the form $an + b$ where a and b are numbers, for example $2n + 3$. ◀ **TOP TIP**

Drawing straight line graphs

To achieve Level 6, you need to be able to draw lines on a graph if given an equation. The *x* and *y* coordinates of every point along a straight line are related and can be described as an equation. You need to be able to plot points to make a straight line.

Let's practise!

Draw the line $y = 2x - 3$.

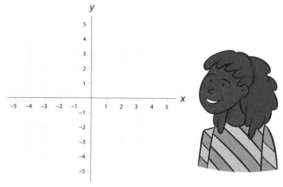

1 Read the question and then read it again.

For every point along the line you draw, the *y* and *x* coordinates are related by the equation $y = 2x - 3$.

2 Choose some values for *x* (e.g. 0, 1, 2, 3) and draw and complete a table.

$y = 2x - 3$

x	0	1	2	3
2*x*	0	2	4	6
−3	−3	−3	−3	−3
$y = 2x - 3$	−3	−1	1	3

3 Write out the coordinates for the *x* and *y* values from your table.

(0, −3) (1, −1) (2, 1) (3, 3)

4 Plot those coordinates on your graph. Use a ruler to join them and continue the line in both directions.

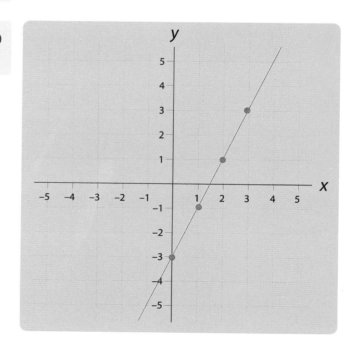

2.

Practice questions

1 Draw the line $y = x + 4$.

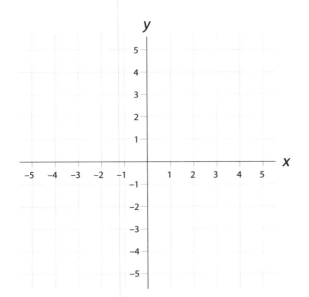

2 Draw the line $y = -2x - 4$.

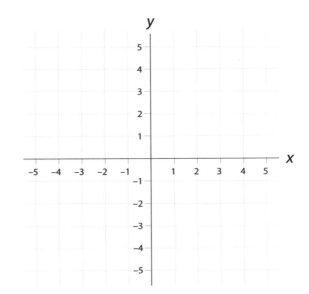

Some equations don't have an x value, for example $y = 4$. These are horizontal lines.

Some equations don't have an y value, for example $x = -2$. These are vertical lines.

Some equations don't have a number after the x, for example $y = 4x$. These lines will go through the origin $(0, 0)$.

Practice questions

Plot these lines on the same graph.

3 $y = 2x - 3$

4 $y = 4$

5 $x = -3$

6 $y = \frac{1}{2}x$

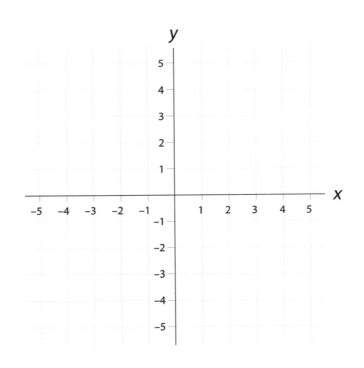

TOP TIP   Choose any values for x to make it easy for yourself!
For question 6, choose even numbers for x to make it easier
to halve, for example choose –2, 0, 2, 4.   **TOP TIP**

Describing straight line graphs

To achieve Level 6, you need to understand how straight line graphs can be described as equations. The x and y coordinates of every point on the straight line are related using the general equation $y = mx + c$. Learn it! (Read the top tips below first to find out about m and c.)

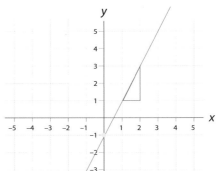

Let's practise!

What is the equation of this line?

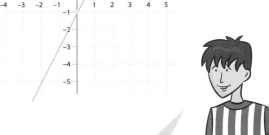

1	Read the question and then read it again.	Find m and c in the equation $y = mx + c$.
2	To find the gradient m, see how many squares you must go up (or down) for every one across you go.	See the red lines above – for one square across you go 2 squares up. The gradient m is 2.
3	Write the gradient into the equation.	$y = 2x + c$
4	Find the y coordinate of the point where the line crosses the y-axis.	See the yellow dot above – it crosses at -1. The intercept c is -1
5	Write out the equation.	$y = 2x + c$ If c is -1, we write $y = 2x - 1$.
6	Pick a point on your line to check your equation.	Choose any point along your line, such as (3, 5). Substitute $x = 3$ and $y = 5$ into $y = 2x - 1$. $5 = 2 \times 3 - 1$. Is this true? Yes!

TOP TIPS

The gradient, m, is how steep a line is.
To measure the gradient, count how many squares you must go up or down for every one square you go across.
If a line slopes up to the right, the gradient is a positive number.
If a line slopes up to the left, the gradient is a negative number.
The point where the line crosses the y-axis (if it does) is called the intercept, c.

TOP TIPS

Practice questions

Write the equations of these lines.

1

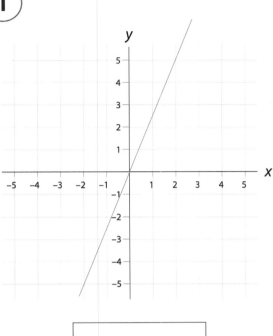

2

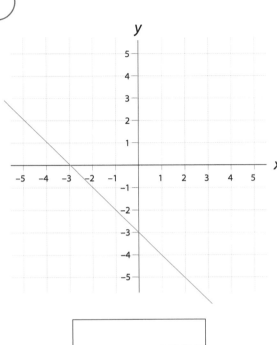

For the gradient of lines that aren't very steep, make a fraction to find *m*.

Example question
Write the equation of the line.

Draw a line going across from a point that crosses two grid lines and then up to another point that does too.
See the red lines.

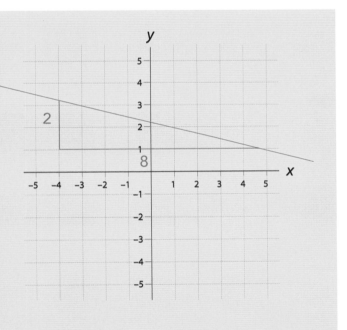

Count how many up: 2
Count how many across: 8

Write the fraction and simplify $\frac{2}{8} = \frac{1}{4}$

So the equation is $y = -\frac{1}{4}x + 2$.
Notice *m* is negative as the line slopes up to the left.

TOP TIP

Always check if *m* is positive or negative. Does it slope up to the right (positive) or left (negative)?
If the line passes through the origin (0, 0) there will be no value for *c*, for example $y = 3x$ or $y = -\frac{1}{2}x$.

TOP TIP

Plans and elevations

To achieve Level 6, you need to be able to draw plans and elevations of solid shapes. A plan of a 3-D shape is the view from above looking down on it. An elevation of a 3-D shape is the view from any of the sides.

Let's practise!

Sketch the plan and an elevation of this cone.

1 Read the question and then read it again.

Remember, a plan is from above and an elevation is from the side.

2 Start with the plan. Sketch it and mark on any vertices or edges that are visible.

Plan:

3 Then draw an elevation. With some shapes there may be several different elevations.

Elevation:

Let's practise!

Which of these three is a plan of a hexagonal prism?

1 Read the question and sketch the 3-D shape in different orientations and with different dimensions.

A hexagonal prism can look like these:

2 Decide which of the given plans matches one of your sketches.

This could be the plan of this 3-D shape:

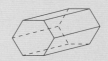

Nets and 2-D representations of 3-D shapes

To achieve Level 6, you need to recognise drawings (2-D representations) of 3-D shapes and be able to sketch nets of them. A net is the unfolded 3-D shape laid flat.

The drawings show some of the ones that you should learn.

There are often many different nets for a single shape, as it can be opened out in different ways. Here are all the nets of a cube:

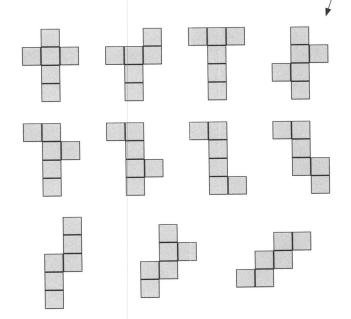

Net of the shape	2-D representation	Net of the shape	2-D representation

TOP TIP   Always count the number of faces of the 3-D shape and make sure your net has the correct number of sections.   **TOP TIP**

37

Quadrilaterals

To achieve Level 6, you need to know the properties and names of quadrilaterals. A quadrilateral is a 2-D shape with four straight sides.

Here are some examples:

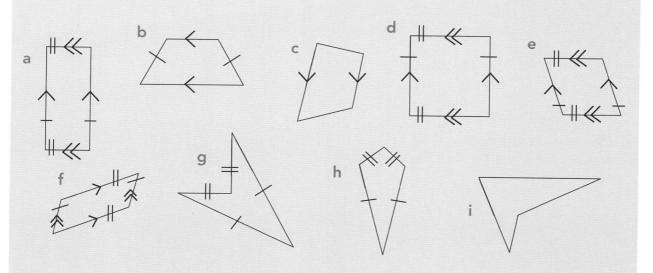

A **parallelogram** has two opposite pairs of parallel lines (shapes a, d, e and f).

A **rectangle** has four right angles. It is a type of parallelogram (shape a).

A **square** has four right angles and four sides of equal length. It is a type of rectangle (shape d).

A **rhombus** has two sets of parallel lines and four sides of equal length. It is a type of parallelogram (shapes e and d). Shape d is a special rhombus – a square.

A **trapezium** has one set of parallel lines (one of the parallel lines is longer than the other) (shapes b and c).

A **kite** has two short sides adjacent and of equal length and two longer ones adjacent and of equal length (shapes g and h). Shape g can also be called an arrowhead.

Shape i is not any of the shapes above, so is just called a **quadrilateral**.

TOP TIP

Arrows are used to show when sides are parallel.
Lines are used to show when sides are equal.

TOP TIP

Let's practise!

Complete the table to show the properties of these quadrilaterals.

Picture	Name of quadrilateral	Number of pairs of parallel sides	Number of pairs of equal sides	Number of right angles
□	square	2	2	
⏢				
▱	rhombus			
◿				

1	Read the question and then read it again.		**Complete the table.**
2	Complete the row for the square.		**A square has 4 right angles so write in: 4**
3	Complete the next row.		**The shape is a trapezium. It has 1 pair of parallel sides and this trapezium has 1 pair of equal sides too. It has no right angles. So write in: trapezium 1 1 0**
4	Complete the next row.		**A rhombus has 2 pairs of parallel sides and 2 pairs of equal sides. This shape has no right angles so write in: 2 2 0**
5	Complete the final row.		**The shape is a kite. It has no parallel sides but 2 pairs of equal sides. This kite has no right angles. Write in: kite 0 2 0**
6	Make sure all sections of the table are complete.		**If not, go back to step 2 and try again.**

TOP TIP   Use your ruler to check whether sides are equal or parallel.   **TOP TIP**

39

Angles of polygons

To achieve Level 6, you need to know about the interior and exterior angles of shapes with straight sides (polygons). The interior angles are those inside the shape. Exterior angles are made by extending the sides of the shape.

An interior and its related exterior angle will always add up to 180°.

Also, all exterior angles of a shape add up to 360°.

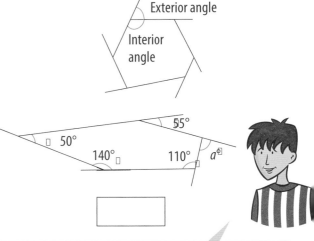

Exterior angle

Interior angle

Let's practise!

Find the value of angle *a*.

1	Read the question and then look carefully at the given information.	Take note: some of the given angles are interior angles and some are exterior angles! We know one exterior angle of 55°.
2	To find exterior angle *a* first find all the other exterior angles.	Subtract any given interior angles from 180° to give the exterior angles. 180° − 110° = 70° 180° − 140° = 40° 180° − 50° = 130°
3	Write out all the exterior angles and find their total.	55°, 70°, 40°, 130° 55° + 70° + 40° + 130° = 295°
4	Subtract this from 360° to find angle *a*.	360° − 295° = 65°
5	If your answer seems sensible, write it in the box.	If not, go back to step 1 and try again.

Practice questions

1. A hexagon has exterior angles of 34°, 36°, 121°, 19°, 26° and *b*°. Find the value of *b*.

2. A polygon has exterior angles of 90°, 80°, 60°, 60° and *c*°. Find the value of *c*.

Sometimes questions may be about the angles in regular polygons.
A regular polygon is a shape with equal sides and equal angles.

Let's practise!

What is the size of each interior angle of a regular octagon?

1	Read the question and then look carefully at the given information.	Remember the exterior angles of any polygon add up to 360°.
2	Ask, 'How many exterior angles does this regular polygon have?'	A regular octagon has eight exterior angles.
3	Divide to find how large each exterior angle is.	$360° \div 8 = 45°$
4	Subtract this from 180° to find angle *a*.	$180° - 45° = 135°$
5	If your answer looks sensible, write it in the box.	If not, go back to step 1 and try again.

Practice questions

1 This is a regular hexagon.
What is the size of angle *b*?

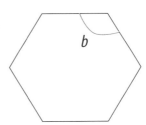

2 Find the size of an interior angle of a regular decagon.

3 Find the sum (total) of all the interior angles of a regular pentagon.

TOP TIP ▶

The exterior angles of any polygon total 360°.
Take care: the total of the interior angles of polygons depends on the number of sides that the shape has.
The interior angles of triangles add up to 180°.
For quadrilaterals they add up to 360°.

◀ **TOP TIP**

Angles between lines

To achieve Level 6, you need to know that when a straight line crosses two parallel lines, some equal angles are formed.

Look out for 'F' or 'Z' shapes. Watch out though as these can be in a rotated or reflected position!

The angles in a 'Z' shape are **equal**. These are called alternate angles.

The angles in an 'F' shape are **equal**. These are called corresponding angles.

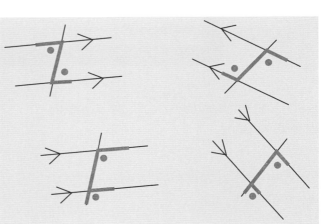

Let's practise!

Find the size of angle *b* in this diagram.

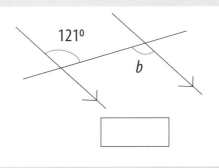

1 Read the question and then read it again.	**What is the size of angle *b*?**
2 Look for alternate or corresponding angles.	**Trace all the different F or Z shapes you can see in the diagram. Look for one that links the given angle and angle *b*.**
3 Picture the shape.	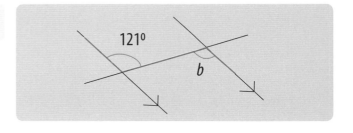
4 Think carefully about which angles are equal.	**The alternate angles show that *b* is equal to 121°.**
5 If your answer looks sensible, write it in the box.	**If not, go back to step 2 and try again.**

Also remember that angles along a straight line have a total of 180° and that where two lines cross the opposite angles are equal.

130°
d c
e
a
g f b
50° h

Let's practise!

Find the sizes of all the missing angles in this diagram.

1. Read the question and then read it again.

What are the sizes of all the angles?

2. Look for alternate or corresponding angles.

Trace all the different F or Z shapes you can see in the diagram to find equal angles.

3. Picture the shapes.

130° and *a* are equal (corresponding angles).

50° and *b* are equal (alternate angles).

Continue like this to find the other angles.

4. Write your answers, looking for patterns to help you check that they are right.

This diagram shows the sizes of all the angles.

130°
50° 50°
130° 130°
50° 50° 130°
130°
50°

Practice questions

1. Find angles c and d

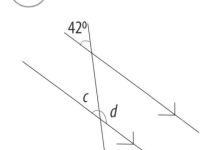

42°

c
d

2. Find angles e and f.

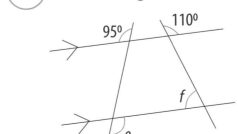

95°
110°

f

e

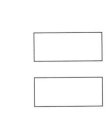

43

Areas of shapes made from rectangles

To achieve Level 6, you need to use know-how to find the areas of rectangles and shapes made from rectangles (called rectilinear shapes). Use this formula:

the area of a rectangle = the length × the width
or $A = l \times w$

Let's practise!

Find the area of this shape made from rectangles.

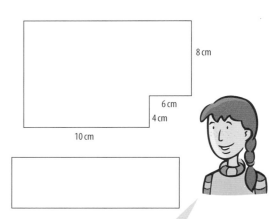

8 cm
6 cm
4 cm
10 cm

1   Read the question and then read it again. | **You are being asked to find the area.**

2   Picture the shape. | **Split the shape into two rectangles.**

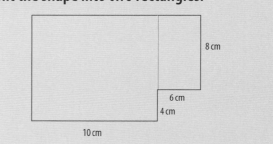

8 cm
6 cm
4 cm
10 cm

3   Remember the formula. | $A = l \times w$

4   Find the area of each rectangle. | **The large rectangle has the length 10 cm and the width 4 cm + 8 cm = 12 cm.**
$A = 10 \times 12 = 120$
For the small rectangle $A = 6 \times 8 = 48$.

5   Add the areas together and write the unit of measurement. | $120 + 48 = 168 \, cm^2$

6   If your answer looks sensible, write it in the box. | **If not, go back to step 2 and try again.**

TOP TIP   When dealing with area, make sure the units are always squared, for example cm^2, m^2, km^2.   **TOP TIP**

The circumference of a circle

To achieve Level 6, you need to work out the circumference of a circle. This is the distance around the edge of the circle, like the perimeter. There are two related formulae you can use:

The circumference is π times the diameter	$C = \pi \times d$ or $C = \pi d$
The circumference is π times 2 lots of the radius	$C = \pi \times 2 \times r$ or $C = 2\pi r$

Let's practise!

Find the circumference of this circle to 2 decimal places (2dp).

7cm

1	Read the question and then read it again.	**Decide whether you have been given the radius or the diameter.**
2	Remember your formula.	**The diameter, 7cm, is given so use $C = \pi d$.**
3	Write the numbers.	$C = \pi \times 7$
4	Key the numbers into your calculator.	[π] [×] [7] [=] 21.99114858
5	Reread the question and write the answer to the appropriate degree of accuracy.	**The question says to give the answer to 2 decimal places, so it is 21.99.**
6	Write in your unit of measurement.	**21.99 cm**
7	If your answer looks sensible, write it in the box.	**The answer should be just over 3 times the length of the diameter.**

TOP TIPS The diameter goes from one edge to the other, passing through the centre.
The radius goes from the centre to the edge.
The diameter is always twice the radius.
Pi or π is a special number about equal to 3.142 or $\frac{22}{7}$. **TOP TIPS**

The area of a circle

To achieve Level 6, you need to work out the area of a circle. This is the amount of space inside the circle. This is the formula to learn:

> the area of a circle is π times the radius squared $A = π \times r \times r$ or $A = πr^2$

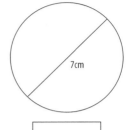

Let's practise!

Find the area of this circle to 1 decimal place (1dp).

7cm

1	Read the question and then read it again.	Decide if you know the radius or the diameter. For area you need the radius, so halve the diameter here. Half of 7 cm = 3.5 cm.
2	Remember your formula.	$A = πr^2$
3	Write the numbers.	$A = π \times 3.5^2$
4	Key the numbers into your calculator.	[π] [×] [3.5] [^2] [=] 38.48451001
5	Reread the question and write the answer to the appropriate degree of accuracy.	The question says to give the answer to 1 decimal place, so it is 38.5.
6	Write in your unit of measurement.	38.5 cm^2
7	If your answer looks sensible, write it in the box.	If not, re-enter it into your calculator.

Practice questions

1 Find the area of a circle with a radius of 5 cm (to 1dp).

2 Find the area of a circle with a diameter of 5 cm (to 1dp).

TOP TIPS   The diameter goes from one edge of the circle to the other, passing through the centre.
The radius goes from the centre to the edge.   **TOP TIPS**
The diameter is always twice the radius.
Pi or π is a special number about equal to 3.142 or $\frac{22}{7}$.

The volume of a cuboid

To achieve Level 6, you need to work out the volume of a cuboid. It's easy – just remember this formula:

> **the volume of a cuboid = the length × the breadth × the height**
> **or $V = l \times b \times h$ or $V = lbh$**

Let's practise!

Find the volume of this cuboid.

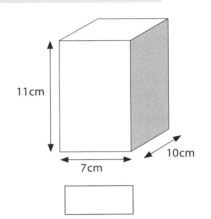

11cm

7cm

10cm

1	Read the question and then read it again.	Take note: you are working with volume, so there may be a formula!
2	Remember your formula.	$V = lbh$
3	Write the numbers.	$V = 7 \times 10 \times 11$
4	Study the numbers and think about them.	It might be easier to rearrange them: $V = 7 \times 10 \times 11 = 7 \times 11 \times 10$
5	Calculate your answer.	$V = 7 \times 11 \times 10 = 77 \times 10 = 770$
6	Write in your unit of measurement.	cm cubed (cm³) = 770 cm³
7	If your answer looks sensible, write it in the box.	If not, go back to step 2 and try again.

TOP TIP

When dealing with volume, make sure the units are always cubed, for example cm³, m³, km³.

Breadth is another word for width.

When a formula has letters next to each other, such as *lbh*, it means that they are multiplied together: $l \times b \times h$.

TOP TIP

Transformations

Transformations are ways of changing shapes, such as reflections, rotations and translations. To achieve Level 6, you need to recognise how shapes have been transformed.

To **reflect** a shape, you need a mirror line. Mirror lines can be horizontal, vertical or diagonal.

Translation just means move or slide without turning. A translation can be horizontal, vertical or diagonal.

A translation of (0, –3) means 0 squares to the right and 3 squares down.
A translation of (–1, 4) means 1 square to the left and 4 squares up.

For a **rotation** you need a **centre of rotation**. The centre of rotation can be inside a shape, on one of its edges or even outside the shape. Then you turn the shape through the angle you are given.

Practice questions

Describe the single transformation that will map:

1 A onto B.

2 C onto D.

3 D onto F.

4 A onto F.

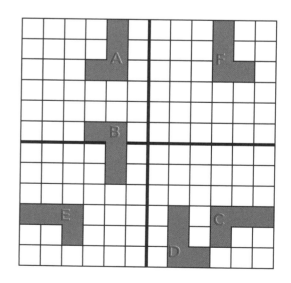

TOP TIPS When describing transformations give as much detail as you can. For reflections give the equation for the mirror line, for example x = 1 or y = 3. For rotations give the angle, its direction (clockwise, etc.) and the coordinates of the centre of rotation. **TOP TIPS**

Enlarging shapes

To achieve Level 6, you need to be able to enlarge a shape by a positive whole number scale factor. An enlargement of a shape changes the size of it. Enlarging with the scale factor 2 makes every side of the shape twice as long. Enlarging with the scale factor 3 makes every side of the shape three times as long and so on.

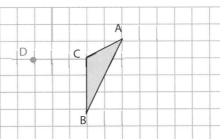

Let's practise!

Enlarge triangle ABC by a scale factor of 3 using the centre of enlargement D.

(1) Read the question and then read it again.

You must enlarge the shape by a scale factor of 3.

(2) Draw lines from the centre of enlargement D, through each vertex and beyond.

Draw the blue lines as shown below.

(3) Find the distance from D to each vertex.

Sometimes you can count this, but sometimes it is easier to use a ruler to measure.
D to C is 3 squares.
D to B is the diagonals of 3 squares.
D to A is 5.1 cm with a ruler.

(4) Multiply each distance by 3. These are the measurements from D to the new vertices.

D to C^1 is 9 squares.
D to B^1 is the diagonals of 9 squares.
D to A^1 is 15.3 cm with a ruler.

(5) Mark these new points on the grid and label them A^1, B^1 and C^1.

(6) Join up the new vertices to make the new shape.

(7) Measure the lengths of the new shape to check that they are 3 times the lengths of the original shape.

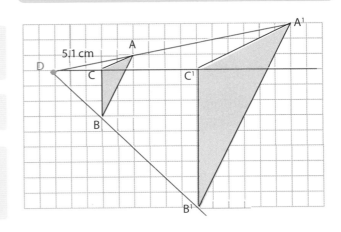

Frequency diagrams

To achieve Level 6, you need to group data into equal class intervals (groups) and plot them as a frequency diagram.

Birth weights in ounces
120, 113, 128, 123, 108, 136, 138, 132, 120, 143, 140, 144, 141, 110,
114, 115, 92, 115, 144, 119, 105, 115, 137, 122, 131, 103, 146, 114,
125, 114, 122, 93, 130, 119, 113, 134, 107, 134, 122, 128, 129, 110,
138, 111, 87, 143, 155, 110, 122, 145

Let's practise!

This raw data shows the birth weights of 50 babies. Group the data into equal class intervals and plot the information into a frequency table.

(1) Read the question and then read it again.

You must group the data first.

(2) Look for the highest and lowest values.

The highest value is 155 and the lowest is 87.

(3) Decide how you could make between 5 and 7 equal class intervals that cover that range.

Perhaps groups of 20 would work, for example 80 to 100, 100 to 120, 120 to 140, 140 to 160. You must make sure the groups don't overlap though!
Write them like this: $80 \leq B < 100$ where B is the birth weight.

(4) Draw a frequency (tally) chart for the data:

Birth weights (B) in ounces	Tally	Frequency
$80 \leq B < 100$		
$100 \leq B < 120$		
$120 \leq B < 140$		
$140 \leq B < 160$		

(5) Carefully work through the list of birth weights, marking a tally for each in your table.

Cross off each weight as you go.

(6) Count up the tallies and write the totals in the frequency column.

Check the frequencies have the total 50.

Once the data are in a frequency table it can be drawn as a frequency diagram:

Birth weights (B) in ounces	Tally	Frequency
$80 \leq B < 100$	\ //	3
$100 \leq B < 120$	++++ ++++ ++++ (//	18
$120 \leq B < 140$	++++ ++++ ++++ ++++	20
$140 \leq B < 160$	++++ ((//	9

7 Plot the frequency along the *y*-axis and the class intervals along the *x*-axis.

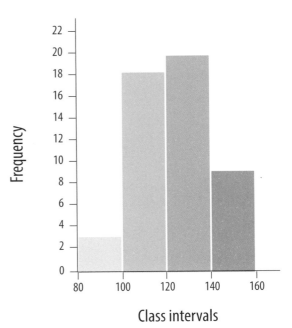

8 Mark the top centre of each bar and then join the marks.

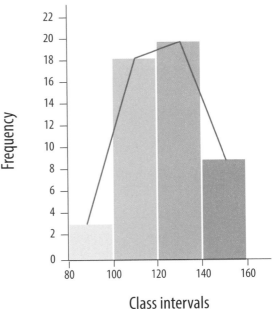

TOP TIP You don't need to draw the bars on first – you can just plot the red line to draw the frequency diagram. **TOP TIP**

Scatter graphs

To achieve Level 6, you need to understand scatter graphs. Scatter graphs show whether there is a connection between two sets of values.

A scatter graph could show:
- **that one value increases as the other increases** (positive correlation)
- **that one value increases as the other decreases** (negative correlation)
- **no connection at all** (zero correlation).

The arrangement of the crosses on the graph show whether the correlation is positive, negative or zero.

Positive	Negative	Zero
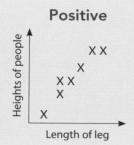	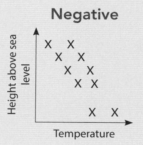	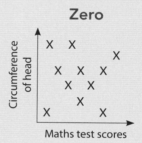

Practice questions
Describe the correlation for each scatter graph.

1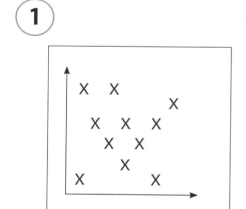

2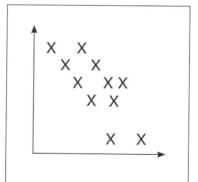

3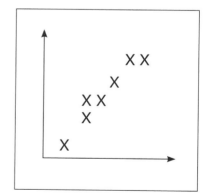

At Level 6 you may also need to plot points to draw your own scatter graphs.

The number of ice creams sold by a seaside shop and the average temperature

Average temperature (°C)	0	5	10	15	20	25	30
Number of ice creams sold	4	7	6	11	25	29	40

Let's practise!

Draw a scatter graph of this information and describe any correlation.

1 Read the question and then read it again.

You must draw a scatter graph and describe the correlation.

2 Draw the graph, plotting the points carefully. Label the axes and give your graph a title.

On squared paper draw and label appropriate axes. Think carefully about the scale you will use on each axis.

A scatter graph to show average temperature against number of ice creams sold

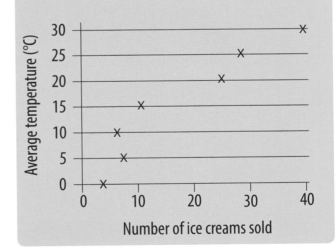

3 Reread the question.

You must also describe the correlation. Here there is some positive correlation but it would be more conclusive if more data were given.

TOP TIP ▶ The more data you have, the more reliably you can describe the correlation. ◀ TOP TIP

Pie charts

To achieve Level 6, you need to draw your own pie charts. The important thing to remember is to find out what angle will represent each person or item. Find the angle by dividing 360° by the number of people or items that the pie chart will represent in total.

Angle for one = 360° ÷ the total number of things represented

This data show the activities or items that 100 twelve-year-old boys spend the largest part of their pocket money on.

Activity or item	Number of boys
Sports and hobbies	45
Going out	10
CDs, videos, DVDs	18
Clothes	9
Computer games	11
Other	7

Let's practise!

Draw a pie chart of this information.

1 Read the question and then read it again. What is the total number of people represented?

It says 100 boys.

2 Divide 360° by the total number of people to find what angle one of them will represent.

360° ÷ 100 = 3.6°
Each boy will be shown by 3.6 degrees.

3 Multiply to find the angle for each slice of the pie, rounding if necessary.

For 'sports and hobbies' multiply 45 by 3.6, etc.

Check that the angles total 360°.

Angle of slice
162°
36°
64.8 → 65°
32.4 → 32°
39.6 → 40°
25.2 → 25°

4 Then use a protractor to help you complete the slices of the pie chart. Label the slices or add a key.

What 100 twelve-year-old boys spent the largest part of their pocket money on

- ▢ Sports and hobbies
- ▪ Going out
- ▢ CDs, videos, DVDs
- ▢ Clothes
- ▪ Computer games
- ▢ Other

Probability: outcomes

To achieve Level 6, you need to work out all the possible outcomes of an event (sometimes called the sample space).

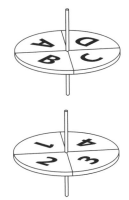

Let's practise!

List all the possible outcomes if these two spinners are spun. How many possible outcomes are there?

1 Read the question and then read it again.

You must list all the possible outcomes.

2 Draw a table or a tree diagram to show the outcomes.

Table

	A	B	C	D
1	A1	B1	C1	D1
2	A2	B2	C2	D2
3	A3	B3	C3	D3
4	A4	B4	C4	D4

Tree diagram
Spinner A, B, C, D   Spinner 1, 2, 3, 4

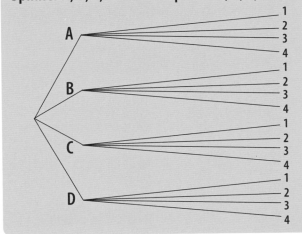

3 Reread the question.

There are 16 possible outcomes.

4 If your answer looks sensible, write it in the box.

If not, go back to step 2 and try again.

Mutually exclusive events

To achieve Level 6, you need to know that mutually exclusive events cannot happen at the same time. Remember this rule: the probabilities of mutually exclusive events always have a total of 1.

Let's practise!

The probability of it raining today is $\frac{3}{10}$. What is the probability of it not raining?

1	Read the question and then read it again.	Read it carefully.
2	Ask: *'Are the events mutually exclusive?'*	It might rain or it might not rain. Yes, they are mutually exclusive.
3	Remember the rule.	The probabilities of mutually exclusive events always have a total of 1.
4	Study the numbers and think about them.	The probability of it not raining is $1 - \frac{3}{10}$
5	Calculate your answer.	$1 - \frac{3}{10} = \frac{7}{10}$
6	If your answer looks sensible, write it in the box.	$P\,(\text{not raining}) = \frac{7}{10}$

Practice questions

1 The probability of rolling a 6 on a dice is $\frac{1}{6}$. What is the probability of not rolling a 6?

2 P (a player will win a tennis match) = 0.6. What is the probability that the player will not win?

Using and applying maths

Throughout this book you have been asked questions that involve using and applying the maths that you know. As part of Level 6 work, you need to solve puzzles and problems related to number, algebra, measures, shape and space, and handling data. Use this flow chart when solving such problems.

Let's practise!

1 Read the question and then read it again.

Read the question carefully – twice. Let the words and numbers 'sink in'.

2 Picture the problem and note or highlight key numbers and words.

It might help to draw a picture or diagram to visualise the problem more clearly.

3 Think about the steps you might follow.

Sometimes you might use trial and improvement strategies. Sometimes it might be best to simplify by starting with smaller numbers or perhaps by breaking the problem into smaller parts. You might even be able to use an equation or formula to help you solve it.

4 Work through your steps systematically.

Check each stage as you go.

5 When you have found a solution or solutions, put them back into the original question to check.

Reread the question, substituting the solution and making sure it works.

6 If your answer looks sensible, write it in the box.

If not, go back to step 2 and try again.

TOP TIPS

TOP TIPS

Remember your 'checking the answer' skills.
Think clearly and *write* clearly.
Present your work so that it shows what you have done.
Work *step by step*.
Make a problem easier by breaking it into smaller steps.
Make estimates when you can.
Look for patterns in your maths.
Persevere! If your method isn't working, change it.
Try something else.

Using and applying maths: number and algebra

Here are some more Level 6 puzzles and problems to try to solve.
Use the flow chart on page 57 to help you.

Practice questions

1 $a + b + c = 30$
$a + b \quad = 22$
$\quad b + c = 14$

What are the values of a, b and c?

[ ] [ ] [ ]

2 A dragon doubles in size every day. After 24 days the dragon fills the cave. After how many days did he half fill the cave? [ ]

3 Fill in the missing numbers:

a) $\dfrac{\boxed{}}{120} = 0.3$

b) $\dfrac{24}{\boxed{}} = 48$

4 Solve these problems:
a) In a field there are y cows and 6 people. There are 52 legs in the field. How many cows are there?

[ ]

b) In a park there are b dogs and 7 people. There are 50 legs in the park. How many dogs are there?

[ ]

c) In a cellar there are t spiders and 4 people. There are 64 legs in the cellar. How many spiders are there?

[ ]

Using and applying maths: shape, space and measures

More practice questions

(5) A jewellery shop makes brooches made from wire. Find the amount of wire used for this brooch to 1dp. Each diameter is 1.5 cm.

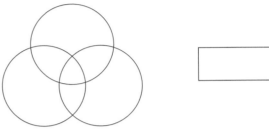

(6) How many sides has a regular polygon that has exterior angles of 24°?

(7) How many sides has a regular polygon that has interior angles of 162°?

(8) A circle with a radius of 6 cm fits inside a square so that it touches the perimeter at four points. Find the total area of the red regions to the nearest whole number.

TOP TIPS
Look back through the book to remind yourself of each topic, to help you.
For question 8, think about how the radius and diameter of the circle are related to the length of the sides of the square.
Remember to write any units of measurement in your answers.
TOP TIPS

Level 6 learning objectives

The following shows you what is required in order for you to achieve Level 6 maths.

Add and subtract fractions and mixed numbers: add and subtract fractions by writing them with a common denominator.

Fraction, decimal and percentage equivalents: understand and use the equivalences between fractions, decimals and percentages, and calculate using ratios in appropriate situations.

Percentage change: understand and use the equivalences between fractions, decimals and percentages, and calculate using ratios in appropriate situations.

Writing a number as a percentage or fraction of another: be aware of which number to consider as 100%, or a whole, in problems involving comparisons, and use this to evaluate one number as a fraction or percentage of another.

Using ratios to divide amounts: understand and use the equivalences between fractions, decimals and percentages, and calculate using ratios in appropriate situations.

Proportional reasoning: understand and use the equivalences between fractions, decimals and percentages, and calculate using ratios in appropriate situations.

Adding or subtracting negative numbers: add or subtract negative numbers.

Using formulae: understand and use appropriate formulae

Trial and improvement: order and approximate decimals when solving numerical problems and equations (e.g. $x^3 + x = 20$), using trial and improvement methods.

Solving simple linear equations: formulate and solve linear equations with whole-number coefficients.

Expanding brackets: formulate and solve linear equations (including brackets) with whole-number coefficients.

Finding the rule for the nth term of a sequence: when exploring number sequences, find and describe in words the rule for the next term or n^{th} term of a sequence where the rule is linear.

Drawing straight line graphs: represent mappings expressed algebraically, and use Cartesian coordinates for graphical representation interpreting general features.

Plans and elevations: recognise and use common 2-D representations of 3-D objects.

Nets and 2-D representations of 3-D shapes: recognise and use common 2-D representations of 3-D objects.

Quadrilaterals: know and use the properties of quadrilaterals in classifying different types of quadrilateral.

Angles of polygons: solve problems using angle and symmetry properties of polygons and explain these properties.

Angles between lines: solve problems using angle properties of intersecting and parallel lines, and explain these properties.

Areas of shapes made from rectangles: understand and use appropriate formulae for finding areas of plane rectilinear figures when solving problems.

The circumference of a circle: understand and use appropriate formulae for finding circumferences of circles when solving problems.

The area of a circle: understand and use appropriate formulae for finding areas of circles when solving problems.

The volume of a cuboid: understand and use appropriate formulae for finding volumes of cuboids when solving problems.

Transformations: enlarge shapes by a positive whole-number scale factor.

Enlarging shapes: enlarge shapes by a positive whole-number scale factor.

Frequency diagrams: collect and record continuous data, choosing appropriate equal class intervals over a sensible range, to create frequency tables. Then construct and interpret frequency diagrams.

Scatter graphs: draw conclusions from scatter diagrams, and have a basic understanding of correlation.

Pie charts: construct pie charts.

Probability – outcomes: when dealing with a combination of two experiments, identify all the outcomes, using diagrammatic, tabular or other forms of communication.

Mutually exclusive outcomes: know that the total probability of all the mutually exclusive outcomes of an experiment is 1.

Using and applying maths: solve problems and carry through substantial tasks by breaking them into smaller, more manageable tasks.

Using and applying maths – number and algebra: using a range of efficient techniques, methods and resources, including ICT, give solutions to an appropriate degree of accuracy.

Using and applying maths – shape, space and measures: interpret, discuss and synthesise information presented in a variety of mathematical forms using symbols, diagrams, graphs and related explanatory texts.

ANSWERS

Answers

Negative numbers (page 10)
1. 27°C
2. 21°C
3. 17°C

Long division (page 11)
1. 48
2. 36
3. 34

Formulae (page 13)
1. $P = 50 + 20N$

Adding and subtracting fractions and mixed numbers (page 17)
1. $1\frac{2}{15}$ or $\frac{17}{15}$
2. $\frac{7}{12}$
3. $1\frac{6}{35}$ or $\frac{41}{35}$
4. $\frac{17}{40}$
5. $\frac{1}{35}$
6. $1\frac{7}{40}$ or $\frac{47}{40}$
7. $8\frac{5}{21}$
8. $2\frac{7}{10}$
9. $1\frac{13}{15}$
10. $2\frac{5}{8}$

Percentage change (page 19)
1. £45.76
2. 17,120,000 or 17.12 million
3. 48,300

Writing a number as a fraction or percentage of another (pages 20–21)
1. $\frac{1}{4}$; 25%
2. $\frac{1}{5}$; 20%
3. $\frac{1}{25}$; 4%
4. $\frac{2}{5}$; 40%
5. $\frac{1}{8}$; 12.5%

Using ratios to divide amounts (page 22)
1. £9; £18; £27
2. £60; £80; £140

Proportional reasoning (page 23)
1. 1050
2. 1000 g or 1 kg
3. 3.4 km

Using formulae (page 25)
1. 77°F
2. $s = 19$

Trial and improvement (page 27)
1. 4.1
2. 2.7
3. 1.8

Solving simple linear equations (page 29)
1. $y = 7$
2. $r = 2$
3. $n = 7$
4. $m = 7$
5. $y = 7$
6. $m = 6$

Expanding brackets (page 30)
1. $12 + 3m$
2. $7y + 7z$
3. $8a + 12b$
4. $10m - 35$
5. $m = 4$
6. $y = 3$

63

Answers

AR

Drawing straight lines (page 33)

1.

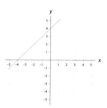

2.

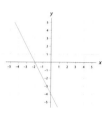

3–6

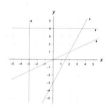

Describing straight line graphs (page 35)

1. $y = 2\frac{1}{2}x$

2. $y = -x - 3$

Angles of polygons (pages 40–41)

1. 124°
2. 70°
3. 120°
4. 144°
5. 540°

Angles between lines (page 43)

1. $c = 42°$; $d = 138°$
2. $e = 95°$; $f = 70°$

The area of a circle (page 46)

1. 78.5 cm²
2. 19.6 cm²

Transformations (page 48)

1. Reflection in the line $y = 2$
2. Anticlockwise rotation of 90 degrees about the point (3, –5)
3. Translation (2, 9)
4. Reflection in the line $x = 1$

Scatter graphs (page 52)

1. zero (or no) correlation
2. negative correlation
3. positive correlation

Mutually exclusive events (page 56)

1. $\frac{5}{6}$
2. 0.4

Using and applying maths: number and algebra (page 58)

1. $a = 16$; $b = 6$; $c = 8$
2. 23 days
3. 36, 0.5 or $\frac{1}{2}$
4. $4y + 12 = 52$, so $y = 10$
   $4b + 14 = 50$, so $b = 9$
   $8t + 8 = 64$, so $t = 7$

Using and applying maths: shape, space and measures (page 59)

5. 14.1 cm
6. 15 sides
7. 20 sides
8. 31 cm²